MW00579572

I dedicate this book to my wife,
Nancy,
who loves to pray.

Special thanks to

- Mike O'Connor
- Jeanette Urato
- Rachel Hass

for their encouragement and editorial insight.

- Sarah Barlow

for the cover design.

Scriptures are taken from various texts:

- NLT—New Living Translation
- NKJV—New King James Version
- NIV—New International Version
- With no attribution it is a paraphrase of the author.

ISBN: 978-0-9971678-3-2

Prayer Is...

Beginning The Adventure Of Prayer

by
Joseph Barlow

A Publication of
Joseph Barlow Ministries
www.josephbarlow.com

Luke 18:1

*...men ought always to pray
and not give up*

Prayer Is...

By Joseph Barlow

Friends, I've written this short book to encourage you in your relationship with God.

Prayer is a part of that relationship. If we strengthen that relationship then prayer is easier and more effective.

Knowing God personally and intimately should be our first goal of prayer. After that, petitions, praise and many prayer adventures await.

Please don't just read this book once but keep it handy as a reminder that God is ready and waiting to connect with you!

I'm praying for you!
Pastor Joe

Section 1:

Sayings About Prayer To Inform, Encourage and Motivate You

Psalms 5:3 NLT

Listen to my voice in the morning, Lord...

Prayer is
your invitation
to fellowship with
God.

John 15:14

...Now you are my friends, since I have told you everything the Father told me.

Prayer is
your invitation
to friendship with
God.

Psalm 86:1

Lord hear my prayer;
answer me, for I need your help.

Prayer is finally turning to the One who can really help you.

Deuteronomy 31:6

...God won't fail you nor abandon you.

Prayer is
knowing there's
Someone there
listening,
even if you
feel completely
alone.

Matthew 6:6

But when you pray,
get by yourself,
shut the door behind you,
and pray to your Father in secret.
Then your God, your Father,
who sees everything,
will reward you.

*Prayer is
sitting
in the presence
of the One
who made you
and loves you.*

1 John 4:8 NLT

But anyone
who does not love
does not know God,
for God is love.

Prayer is communing with Love itself.

John 15:15 NLT

I no longer call you slaves,
because a master doesn't confide
in his slaves.
Now you are my friends,
since I have told you everything
the Father told me.

Prayer is
talking
with a Friend.

Ephesians 1:18 NLT

I pray
that your hearts will be flooded
with light
so that you can understand
the confident hope
he has given to those he called -
his holy people
who are his rich
and glorious inheritance.

Prayer is
listening
to the heart
of the One
who made you.

Luke 12:32 NLT

*"So don't be afraid, little flock.
For it gives your Father
great happiness
to give you
the Kingdom."*

*Prayer is
cuddling
on God's lap,
whispering
your desires
in His ear.*

Isaiah 56:7 NLT

I will bring them
to my holy mountain of Jerusalem
and will fill them with joy
in my house of prayer.
I will accept their burnt offerings and sacrifices,
because my Temple
will be called a house of prayer
for all nations.

Prayer is enjoyable.

John 14:14 NLT

Yes,
ask me for anything in my name,
and I will do it!

*Prayer is
going to get
what you need
from a Friend
who is glad
to give it.*

Matthew 11:28 NLT

Then Jesus said,
Come to me,
all of you who are weary
and carry heavy burdens,
and I will give you rest.

Prayer is lightening your heavy load.

Philippians 4:19 NLT

And this same God
who takes care of me
will supply all your needs
from his glorious riches,
which have been given to us
in Christ Jesus.

Prayer is
like going into the
storehouse
to get
whatever
you need.

Mark 1:35 NLT

Before daybreak
the next morning,
Jesus got up
and went out to an isolated place
to pray.

Prayer is
where we receive
heaven's
sustenance,
direction,
and support.

John 14:1 NKJV

Let not your heart be troubled;
You believe in God,
Believe also in Me.

Prayer is
flying
above
the circumstances
not entangled.

Daniel 2:22 NLT

He reveals
deep and mysterious things
and knows
what lies hidden in darkness,
though he is surrounded
by light.

Prayer is
gaining insight
from
the Revealer
of Secrets.

1 John 3:8b NLT

But the Son of God
came to destroy
the works of the devil.

*Prayer is
the weapon
the Enemy
fears the most.*

John 14:3 NLT

When everything is ready,
I will come and get you,
so that you
will always be with me
where I am.

Prayer is defined by relationship.

Isaiah 41:10 NLT

Don't be afraid,
for I am with you!
Don't be discouraged,
for I am your God.
I will strengthen you and help you.
I will hold you up
with my victorious right hand.

Prayer is
Jesus
coming
to the rescue.

Romans 12:2 NLT

Don't copy the behavior and customs
of this world,
but let God transform you
into a new person
by changing the way you think.
Then you will learn to know
God's will for you,
which is good and pleasing and perfect.

Prayer is
like
going into
the war room,
all the plans
and authority
are there.

Psalms 18:1 NLT

I love you, Lord;
you are my strength.

Prayer is telling God you love Him.

1 John 4:16 NLT

We know how much God loves us,
and we have put our trust in his love.
God is love,
and all who live in love
live in God,
and God lives in them.

Prayer is letting God tell you He loves you.

Psalms 118:5 NLT

In my distress
I prayed to the Lord,
and the Lord answered me...

*Prayer is
like eating
a good meal:
you leave
satisfied.*

Colossians 2:3 NLT

In him lie hidden
all the treasures
of wisdom and knowledge.

Prayer is
getting counsel
from
Someone
who really does
know
everything!

Psalms 100:4 NLT

Enter his gates with thanksgiving;
go into his courts with praise.
Give thanks to him
and praise his name.

Prayer is
God's office door
open
to you.

Matthew 7:7 NLT

"Keep on asking,
and you will receive what you ask for."

Prayer is not begging. It is asking in trust.

1 John 1:9 NKJV

If we confess our sins,
He is faithful and just
to forgive us our sins
and to cleanse us
from all unrighteousness.

Prayer is cleansing to the soul.

1 Corinthians 1:4 NLT

I always thank my God for you
and for the gracious gifts
he has given you,
now that you belong to Christ Jesus.

Prayer is
God's grace
loosed
on your life.

Psalms 145:18 NLT

The Lord is close
to all who call on him,
yes, all who call on him in truth.

*Prayer is
where
the watchman
is friends
with the King.*

Matthew 21:22 NLT

"You can pray for anything,
and if you have faith,
you will receive it."

Prayer is you victorious.

Mark 11:25 NLT

*"But when you are praying,
first forgive anyone
you are holding a grudge against,
so that your Father in heaven
will forgive your sins, too."*

Prayer is
you
forgiven.

Jeremiah 33:3 NLT

Ask me
and I will tell you
remarkable secrets
you do not know
about things to come.

*Prayer is
seeing
what
He reveals
to you.*

Romans 8:26

And the Holy Spirit
helps us in our weakness.
We don't know
How God wants us to pray
But the Holy Spirit prays through us...

Prayer is
the Holy Spirit
at work.

Revelation 3:20 KJV

Behold,
I stand at the door, and knock:
if any man hear my voice,
and open the door,
I will come in to him,
and will sup with him,
and he with me.

*Prayer is
an invitation
to tea
with
the Maker
of the universe.*

Jeremiah 29:11 NLT

"For I know the plans I have for you,"
say the Lord.
"They are plans for good
and not for disaster,
to give you a future and a hope."

Prayer is hope-filled.

Jeremiah 33:3 NKJV

Call to Me,
and I will answer you,
and show you
great and mighty things,
which you do not know.

Prayer is being one with the God-to-Man flow.

Psalm 55:22 NKJV

Cast your burden on the Lord,
And He shall sustain you;
He shall never permit
the righteous to be moved.

Prayer is relieving.

Ephesians 1:23 NLT

And the church is his body;
it is made full
and complete by Christ,
who fills all things
everywhere
with himself.

Prayer is refilling.

Proverbs 15:8 NLT

The Lord
detests the sacrifice
of the wicked,
but he delights in
the prayers of the upright.

Prayer is good.

Jeremiah 29:12 NLT

In those days when you pray,
I will listen.

Prayer is
the umbilical cord
of Heaven.

Jude 20 NKJV

But you,
beloved,
building yourselves up
in your most holy faith,
praying in the Holy Spirit.

Prayer is
like
high power lines.

1 John 3:1a NLT

See how very much
our Father loves us,
for he calls us his children,
and that is what we are!

*Prayer is
a comfortable
conversation
between
a confident child
and
an approving
Father.*

Mark 11:23 NKJV

For assuredly, I say to you,
whoever says to this mountain,
'Be removed and be cast into the sea,'
and does not doubt in his heart,
but believes that those things
he says will be done,
he will have whatever he says.

*Prayer is
letting
the voice of God
flow through you
with
His authority.*

Ezekiel 28:2a NLT

"Son of man,
give the prince of Tyre
this message from the Sovereign Lord..."

Prayer is speaking from Heaven, and Satan knows it's not you!

Genesis 1:28 NLT

Then God blessed them and said,
"Be fruitful and multiply.
Fill the earth
and govern it.
Reign over the fish in the sea,
the birds in the sky,
and all the animals
that scurry along the ground."

Prayer is
yielding
your voice
to the
language
of Heaven
to overcome
Earth's darkness.

Jeremiah 1:5 NLT

"Before you were born
I set you apart
and appointed you
as my prophet to the nations."

Prayer is
being
the mouthpiece
of God.

3 John 4 NKJV

I have no greater joy
than to hear that my children
walk in truth.

Prayer is
you
speaking
from His throne,
in His name;
and He smiles.

Hebrews 4:16 NLT

So let us come boldly
to the throne of our gracious God.
There we will receive his mercy,
and we will find grace
to help us when we need it most.

Prayer is
confidently
laughing
at Earth's realities
armed
with
a Friendship.

Ephesians 2:6

And God raised us up
with Christ
and seated us
with Himself
in the heavenly realms
in Christ Jesus,

Prayer is
where we get to
spend as much
time as we want
with our loving
Heavenly Father,
Jesus Christ Our
Savior and the
Precious Holy
Spirit!

Acts 1:14 NLT

They all met together
and were constantly
united in prayer,
along with Mary the mother of Jesus,
several other women,
and the brothers of Jesus.

Prayer is where you belong.

Greetings,

I hope you've been enjoying this book so far.

That first section has many items you can go back and read over and again.

This next section contains quotes from my journal, where I was communing with God and He spoke things into my heart. I wrote them down and felt that they could be helpful to you.

If that intrigues you, that someone could actually hear God speaking to them and transcribe His words, then I encourage you join the class

"Hearing The Voice of God & Journaling".

You can learn more about this at www.josephbarlow.com.
Blessings
Joe

Pastor Joseph Barlow

Section 2:

Words
From The Lord
For You
To Ponder
And
Meditate

Child,
receive my best.
I am an abundant God
and I have
abundance for you.
I can grant
what you request.

Make way for me
by making requests
of what you'd
like me to do.
I delight in
answering
your prayers.

I've developed
the system,
it works well.

I didn't design prayer
to have it
not work.

I created it.
It works.

Pursue me Son.

Press deeper
into knowing me.
Press deeper into
enjoying me,
learning more fully
who I am
and how close
I desire to be to you.

Son,
there are
many aspects
of my character and
personality that are still
unrevealed to you. Yet I
invite you to come and
get to know
me.

Come.

I put a confidence
in man
that his voice is heard
by my ears.
I built this into man.
He has a knowing
that his voice
is heard on high.

I put a confidence in
man that
I hear his prayers…

For this to be
absent in man,
it must be
trained out of him.

Prayer is in
every culture.
Not one lacks this.

Man
is
naturally
a pray-er.

Child,
I'm with you.
I'm not
your enemy.
I'm your friend.
Don't avoid me.
Just talk to me.
I am here.
I have not left.

Connect.

Child,
Why is that
hard for you?
Are you hiding?
Ashamed?
Guilty?
Fearful?
Search your heart Child.
Come close.
Let me speak.

Son,
this time with Me
is more important
than any other.

Cling to it.
Pursue it.
Plan for it.
Steal away to it.

Just you and Me.

Come.

I have much
for you here,
and I don't want you to
miss a thing.

Fear not.

Boldness
comes from me.

I will speak through you.
And I will accomplish
my purposes.
So do not hold back on
what I would have you
do or say.

Boldness Son.

Boldness!

Son, I'm at work.
Continue to
follow me.
I'll show you
the path.

Pray,
sleep, rest,
read, study, write,
pray,
work, love your family.

Son, all is well.

Section 3:

Scriptures For The Study of Prayer

Author's Note

I love the Word of God.

From it I receive blessing after blessing. While reading the scriptures, I know that I am fellowshipping with God. I'm spending time with Him. I expect Him to be there when I'm reading. I expect Him to speak to my heart while I'm reading.

The next section of this book contains scriptures that will encourage you in prayer. Please set aside the time, take the time to go through them with Him.

Honestly, that is the key to reading the scriptures:

To read it with Him.

Invite the Holy Spirit to speak to you as you read.

What is He trying to say to you about prayer?

There's plenty of room for you to take notes right in this book.

Take the time.

Make the time.

He's worth it.

Again,
I'm praying for you.
Pastor Joe

Pastor Joseph Barlow

Matthew 21:22 NIV

If you believe,
you will receive
whatever
you ask for in prayer.

Isaiah 55:6 NKJV

*Seek the Lord
while he may be found;
call upon him while he is
near*

1 Thessalonians 5:17 NKJV

Pray without ceasing

Psalm 88:13

But I, O Lord,
cry to you;
in the morning
my prayer comes
before you.

Philippians 4:6, 7

Do not be anxious about
anything, but in everything by
prayer and petition
with thanksgiving make your
requests known to God.
7 and the peace of God,
which goes beyond all
understanding,
will guard your hearts and
minds in Christ Jesus.

Luke 11:1 NLT

Now Jesus was praying in a certain place, and when he finished, one of his disciples said to him,

Lord, teach us to pray, as John taught his disciples.

Matthew 6:9-13 NKJV

In this manner, therefore, pray:

Our Father in heaven,
Hallowed be Your name.
10 Your kingdom come
Your will be done
On earth as it is in heaven
11Give us this day our daily bread.
12 And forgive us our debts,
As we forgive our debtors.
13 And do not lead us into temptation,
But deliver us from the evil one.
For Yours is the kingdom and the power
and the glory forever.
Amen.

Ephesians 6:18

Praying
in the Spirit
all the time,
with all kinds of
prayers and petitions.
And keep alert
persevering,
as you pray for
all the saints,

Mark 11:24

*Therefore I tell you,
whatever you
ask for in prayer,
believe that you
have received it,
and it will be yours.*

1 Timothy 2:8

*I desire then
that everywhere
men should pray,
lifting up holy hands
without anger
or quarreling;*

James 5:16

Therefore,
confess your sins
to one another
and pray for one another,
that you may be healed.

The prayers of the
righteous are powerful
and they work!

Psalm 4:1

Answer me when I call,
O God
Who has made me holy!

You helped me before
when I needed you.
Be gracious to me
and hear my prayer!

Hebrews 5:7

When He lived on earth,
Jesus offered up prayers
and petitions,
with loud cries and tears,
to the one who could save
him from death, and God
heard him for his
reverence.

1 John 5:14-15

We have confidence toward
God, that if we ask anything
That lines up with his will
he hears us.
Since we know he hears us
in whatever we ask,
we know that we have
what we have
asked of him.

Psalm 145:18 NKJV

The Lord
is near to all
who call on him,
to all who call upon him
in truth.

Final Thoughts

Friends,

I hope this book has blessed you.

I love to pray because I love God!

Prayer is spending time with Him, fellowshipping, resting, listening.

He's the best Friend anyone could ever have.

If you've not experienced that in your life. Spend time reading this book again and again. See what the Lord does in your heart as you continue to pursue Him.

I've added additional info about myself and the ministry, but most importantly I've added two pages at the end including prayers to lead you into a new life in Christ and to receiving the Baptism of the Holy Spirit.

He loves you so!
Pastor Joe

Pastor Joseph Barlow

Joseph Barlow

Joseph Barlow has been ministry minded most of his life. Since his salvation at 11 and his call to the ministry at 17 he has kept his eyes on God's call for his life.

Joe received his bachelor's degree in Music Theory and Composition, then married Nancy Pictor after she finished her nursing degree.

Seven children have come forth from this blessed marriage, each child a gift from God.

Much business experience was Joe's preparation for ministry along with serving as a worship leader, audio engineer, Music Ministry Coordinator, Bible School Director and staff pastor.

Joe has a call to the nations as well as a mantle of fatherhood. Many seek his counsel on a wide variety of matters.

Joe's musical recordings have ministered to many, his guitar playing, it is said, seems to "open heaven".

Being led by the Spirit is the essential element of Joe's ministry and his life. Romans 8 says, "They that are led by the Spirit are Sons of God."

Drawing people to God, to relationship with Him, to experience Him, to know Him; that's the focus of Joe's life.

The church he founded and pastors, Family Life Christian Center, is a community of believers who are very loving, a great family and very missions minded.

Joseph Barlow Ministries

Joseph Barlow Ministries

This book is a publication of Joseph Barlow Ministries.
The following is a small introduction to our ministry.
You can learn more by going to www.josephbarlow.com.

Our Purpose

- We help you draw closer to God through worship, teaching and discipleship.
- We help you to get filled with the Holy Spirit.
- We teach you how to hear the voice of God for yourself.
- We empower you to fulfill your highest calling in Christ.

Missions

So far I have ministered in: Costa Rica, Honduras, Portugal, Luxembourg, Germany, Angola, Liberia, Uganda, The Philippines and the USA. Preaching, teaching, prophesying and sharing my music.

Music

We have produced several Albums
Available on all major streaming platforms:

- Faithful Is He
- A Day With Jesus
- A Longing Fulfilled
- Talk To Me Lord
- Healing Is Yours
- Know You

Online Classes

- Hearing the Voice of God & Journaling
- Wealth To The Nations
- Fresh Move (Living The Spirit Filled Life)

Pastor Joseph Barlow

Meetings
We do local meetings mostly focused on following the leading of the Holy Spirit. Again, please visit our website at www.josephbarlow.com.

Online Ministry
We try to remain very active in social media to encourage, strengthen and disciple people.
Please consider joining our group Daily Discipleship With Joe Barlow on Facebook.

Books
This book is the second of many.
Our first book is:
Change Is For The Brave
Available on Amazon and www.josephbarlow.com.

Partnership
When God had me start this ministry He said I have not called you to do this alone. You must have partners.
Friend, if God is encouraging you to join us please pray for us and sign up for a monthly gift through www.josephbarlow.com.

God bless
Joe

Joseph Barlow Ministries

Prayer For A New Life

If you could trade the life you've lived so far for the one God designed you for, would you do it?

If the Lord has been tugging at your heart to come closer to Him, it may be time to go ahead and give your whole life to Him.

If you've been weighed down with guilt and are tired of feeling ashamed and disgusted with how things have been going, it may be time! Time to finally say yes to a relationship, a real relationship with God.

He made a way for you to come to Him. He cleared a path. Jesus gave His life to cleanse you from all your sins and make you brand new. Ready?

The Bible says call on the name of the Lord and you will be saved.

Saved from what? Many things. The mess you're in. The future mess you're headed towards, even Hell.

Give your life to Jesus and everything will become new for you.

Pray this now:

Heavenly Father,
I need you. I come to you as a sinner needing a new life.
Forgive me of my sins. Make me brand new.
Give me a new life. Lord, I believe that you raised Jesus from the dead! Jesus you are my Lord. From this day on, God,
I belong to you! My whole life is yours. Let's live it together.
In Jesus name!
Amen!

Pastor Joseph Barlow

Prayer For Power

It seems that Jesus had more power to live victorious than we Christians do. He always had the right answer that blew everybody away. He didn't seem to need to obey natural laws. He walked on water, raised the dead, healed the sick, and fed multitudes with a little boy's lunch.

Are we supposed to imitate Him? Are we supposed to just try to be like Him? Doesn't that seem foolish? It's kind of like a kid with a Superman cape that wants to jump off the roof of the garage. It's cute but definitely not effective.

I think there's a different way. Jesus said, in Acts 1:8 "but you shall receive power when the Holy Ghost comes upon you". In 1 Corinthians 12, it says the Holy Spirit gives us gifts that are beyond human ability. In John chapters 14, 15, & 16 Jesus introduces us to the ministry of the Holy Spirit through you and me.

In the Book of Acts, the Holy Spirit came upon people who were praying. He came upon people when the disciples laid hands on them, but Jesus also promised that God would give the Holy Spirit to those who ask. Are you ready to ask?
The pre-requisite is that you are a believer in Jesus Christ.

Let's pray:

Heavenly Father, I do believe in your Son, Jesus Christ. Jesus is my Lord. So, Father, now I need the same power that Jesus had so that I can imitate Him and live this life as He did.
So, Lord, I ask you to fill me with your Holy Spirit right now.
Holy Spirit you are welcome in my life. Teach me. Lead me.
Draw me closer and closer to God. And use me Lord to do whatever you want to do. I love you, Lord!
In Jesus name,
Amen!

Joseph Barlow Ministries

Made in United States
North Haven, CT
05 October 2023